HEAVEN'S
TOUCH

Cover image *Heavenly Hands* © Greg Olsen. By arrangement with Mill Pond Press, Venice, Florida, 34285. For information on art prints by Greg Olsen, please contact Visions of Faith at 1-800-853-1352.

Cover and book design © 2006 by Covenant Communications, Inc.

Published by Covenant Communications, Inc.
American Fork, Utah

Copyright © 2006 by Covenant Communications, Inc.

Printed in China
First Printing: March 2006

12 11 10 09 08 07 06   10 9 8 7 6 5 4

ISBN 1-59811-086-1

FEATURING ART BY GREG OLSEN

HEAVEN'S

A Tribute to Women

TOUCH

Love

I have learned to place a high estimate upon the love of mother. I have often said, and will repeat it, that the love of a true mother comes nearer being like the love of God than any other kind of love.

JOSEPH F. SMITH, GOSPEL DOCTRINE, 315.

The true spirit of the Church of Jesus Christ of Latter-day Saints gives to woman the highest place of honor in human life. To maintain and to merit this high dignity she must possess those virtues which have always, and which will ever, demand the respect and love of mankind . . . [because] "a beautiful and chaste woman is the perfect workmanship of God."

First Presidency of Heber J. Grant, *Improvement Era*, May 1935, 276.

In my childhood . . . I was instructed to believe in the divinity of the mission of Jesus Christ. I was taught by my mother, a Saint indeed—that Jesus Christ is the Son of God.

JOSEPH F. SMITH, *GOSPEL DOCTRINE*, 1939, 494.

There can be no genuine happiness separate and apart from the home. . . . There is no happiness without service, and there is no service greater than that which converts the home into a divine institution, and which promotes and preserves family life. . . . The strongest attachments of childhood are those that cluster about the home, and the dearest memories of old age are those that call up the associations of youth and its happy surroundings.

JOSEPH F. SMITH, *GOSPEL DOCTRINE*, 1939, 300–01.

Humility

Woman, why weepest thou? whom seekest thou?

John 20:15

Evidence of the Savior's high regard for women is [in] the appearance of the resurrected Lord first to them. He came initially to Mary from Magdala, then appeared to a group of women including Mary, the mother of James; Salome; and others before he presented himself to the brethren.

Russell M. Nelson, "Daughters of Zion," New Era, Nov. 1985, 5.

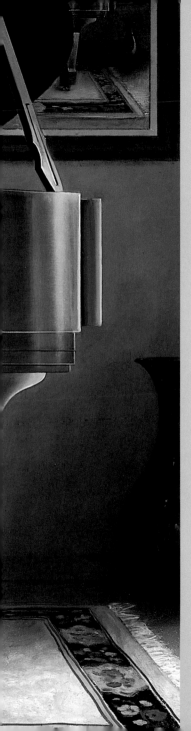

God does notice us, and he watches over us. But it is usually through another person that he meets our needs. Therefore, it is vital that we serve each other in the kingdom.

Spencer W. Kimball, "Small Acts of Service," *Ensign*, Dec. 1974, 5.

A child who under-stands who he is, and who has the kind of home where he feels wanted and loved, has no need to go wandering off to try to find his identity and to search for a happiness he will not find outside the established order of society.

N. Eldon Tanner, "Happiness Is Home Centered," Tambuli, Feb. 1979, 1.

Neither is the man
without the woman,
neither the woman
without the man,
in the Lord.

1 Cor. 11:11

Woman stands at [man's] side a joint-inheritor with him in the fulness of all things. Exaltation and eternal increase is her lot as well as his. Godhood is not for men only; it is for men and women together.

Bruce R. McConkie, Mormon Doctrine, 1966, 844.

The Prophet taught that men and women are of equal value and of equal importance in the sight of God. He preached that in order for a man to achieve his highest potential (the celestial kingdom and godhood) he must have a woman—equally exalted—by his side and sealed to him forever! A just God would not require the yoking of two unequal beings for eternity.

IDA SMITH, "THE LORD AS A ROLE MODEL FOR MEN AND WOMEN," *ENSIGN*, AUG. 1980, 66.

A few years ago I met with a prospective mission president and his wife to discuss their availability for service. I asked whether their responsibilities to aged parents would preclude their service at that time. This sister was the only daughter of a wonderful mother, then about 80, whom she visited and helped each week. Though somewhat dependent physically, this mother was strong spiritually. . . . Because [this mother] was in tune with the Spirit, . . . several months before this interview she told her daughter that the Spirit had whispered that her daughter's husband would be called as a mission president. So advised, the mother had prepared herself for the needed separation and assured her daughter, long in advance of my assignment for the exploratory interview, that she would "not be a hindrance" to their service.

DALLIN H. OAKS, "ALWAYS HAVE HIS SPIRIT," *ENSIGN*, NOV. 1996, 59.

The great strength of a good woman—a Saint, if you will—is her personal testimony of the Savior and her faith in his spokesmen, the prophet and the Apostles of Jesus Christ. If she follows them, she will have the countenance of Christ for her beauty, the peace of Christ to support her emotionally, the Savior's example as a means to solve her problems and to strengthen her, and the love of Christ as the source of love for herself, her family, and those about her. She can be sure of herself as a wife and mother and find joy and fulfillment in her role in the home.

"THE HONORED PLACE OF WOMAN," EZRA TAFT BENSON, *ENSIGN*, NOV. 1981, 104.

A beautiful, modest, gracious woman is creation's masterpiece. When to these virtues a woman possesses as guiding stars in her life righteousness and godliness and an irresistible impulse and desire to make others happy, no one will question if she be classed among those who are truly great.

DAVID O. MCKAY, *GOSPEL IDEALS*, 449.

*W*e are all different. Some are tall, and some are short. Some are round, and some are thin. And almost everyone at some time or other wants to be something they are not! But as one adviser to teenage girls said: "You can't live your life worrying that the world is staring at you. When you let people's opinions make you self-conscious you give away your power . . . The key to feeling [confident] is to always listen to your inner self—[the *real* you.]" And in the kingdom of God, the real you is "more precious than rubies."

Jeffrey R. Holland, "To Young Women," Ensign, Nov. 2005, 28.

Daughter(s), use all your gifts to build up righteousness in the earth.

SUSA YOUNG GATES, *THE LIFE STORY OF BRIGHAM YOUNG*, 1930, 307.

Much of your work as a woman is to enrich mankind. Care and mercy seem to be a dominant refrain of the song you have the opportunity to sing. I hope you will not leave any of the melody unsung.

JAMES E. FAUST, "A MESSAGE TO MY GRANDDAUGHTERS: BECOMING 'GREAT' WOMEN,'"
ENSIGN, SEP. 1986, 16.

Gifts

ultivate and employ generously your noble, womanly instincts of care and mercy, first to your family and then to others. May you always hunger and thirst after righteousness within the framework of the revealed gospel of Jesus Christ. May you have an eternal perspective as you go about your angelic cause of doing good so that it will not only lead you to become great women but ultimately to become queens in the eternities.

JAMES E. FAUST, "HOW NEAR TO THE ANGELS," NEW ERA, MAR. 1999, 4.

One night [a group of Latter-day Saint pioneers] camped in a small valley. After supper they built a big bonfire. They sang and danced around the bonfire to help them forget their fears and worries.

Before they went to bed in their wagons, leaving a single guard on duty, they sang, "Come, Come, Ye Saints," a song they used to encourage each other and show their dedication to the Lord.

That night there were a thousand unfriendly Indians hiding around the camp, ready to attack the pioneers. But after the Indians heard the pioneers sing "Come, Come, Ye Saints," they were unable to attack. They knew the Great Spirit was watching over the pioneers, so they got on their horses and rode away, leaving the pioneers alone.

Some time later, the man who had been chief over the group of Indians told this story to some Latter-day Saint missionaries. When he finished the story, he took out a violin and began to play "Come, Come, Ye Saints." He explained to the missionaries, "This is your song, but it is my song, too. I play it every night before I go to bed. It brings the Great Spirit here to me and makes me and my people calm and happy."

LUCILE C. READING, "SONG OF THE PIONEERS," CHILDREN'S FRIEND, JUL. 1965, 37.

A mother has far greater influence on her children than anyone else, and she must realize that every word she speaks, every act, every response, her attitude, even her appearance and manner of dress affect the lives of her children and the whole family. It is while the child is in the home that he gains from his mother the attitudes, hopes, and beliefs that will determine the kind of life he will live and the contribution he will make to society.

N. Eldon Tanner, "No Greater Honor: The Woman's Role," *New Era*, Jan. 1977, 31.

Kristen was finishing a graduate degree and had recently given birth to her second child. She felt the other graduates had accomplished so much more and was reluctant to attend the graduation dinner. Her fears were confirmed when, at the dinner, the students were asked to list their professional accomplishments.

Kristen recalled: "I suddenly felt embarrassed and ashamed. I had nothing to call myself, no lofty position, no impressive job title." To make matters worse, the professor read the lists as he presented a diploma to each student. The woman ahead of Kristen had many accomplishments: she already had a PhD, was receiving a second master's degree, and she'd even been a mayor! The woman received grand applause.

Then it was Kristen's turn. She handed the professor her blank sheet, trying to hold back the tears. The professor had been one of her teachers and had praised her performance. He looked at her blank paper. Without missing a beat he announced, "Kristen holds the most critical role in all of society." He was quiet for a few seconds, then declared in a powerful voice, "She is the mother of her children." Instead of a few courteous claps, people rose to their feet. There was just one standing ovation that night; it was for the mother in the room.

Bonnie D. Parkin, "Sweet Moments," Ensign, Nov. 2005, 107.

Accomplishment

There are people fond of saying that women are the weaker instruments, but I don't believe it. Physically they may be, but spiritually, morally, religiously, and in faith, what man can match a woman who is really converted to the gospel! Women are more willing to make sacrifices than are men, more patient in suffering, more earnest in prayer. They are the peers and often superior to men in resilience, in goodness, in morality, and in faith.

HUGH B. BROWN, RELIEF SOCIETY CONFERENCE, 29 SEP. 1965.

We must cherish one another, watch over one another, comfort one another and gain instruction, that we may all sit down in heaven together.

LUCY MACK SMITH, *Nauvoo Minutes*, 24 Mar. 1842.

*M*otherhood is near to divinity. It is the highest, holiest service to be assumed by mankind. It places her who honors its holy calling and service next to the angels.

James R. Clark, comp., *Messages of the First Presidency of The Church of Jesus Christ of Latter-day Saints*, 6 vols. (1965–75), 6:178.

Faith

od has given us the capacity to exercise faith, that we may find peace, joy, and purpose in life. However, to employ its power, faith must be founded on something. There is no more solid foundation than faith in the love Heavenly Father has for you, faith in His plan of happiness, and faith in the capacity and willingness of Jesus Christ to fulfill all of His promises.

RICHARD G. SCOTT, "THE SUSTAINING POWER OF FAITH IN TIMES OF UNCERTAINTY AND TESTING," ENSIGN, MAY 2003, 75.

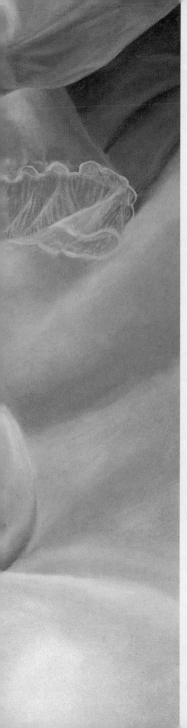

$\mathcal{M}$otherhood is the greatest potential influence either for good or ill in human life. The mother's image is the first that stamps itself on the unwritten page of the young child's mind. It is her caress that first awakens a sense of security; her kiss, the first realization of affection; her sympathy and tenderness, the first assurance that there is love in the world.

DAVID O. MCKAY, GOSPEL IDEALS, 452.

The home is the first and most effective place for children to learn the lessons of life: truth, honor, virtue, self-control; the value of education, honest work, and the purpose and privilege of life. Nothing can take the place of home in rearing and teaching children, and no other success can compensate for failure in the home.

DAVID O. MCKAY, *FAMILY HOME EVENING MANUAL*, 1968, iii.

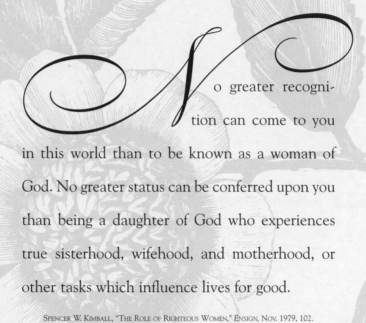

*N*o greater recognition can come to you in this world than to be known as a woman of God. No greater status can be conferred upon you than being a daughter of God who experiences true sisterhood, wifehood, and motherhood, or other tasks which influence lives for good.

Spencer W. Kimball, "The Role of Righteous Women," *Ensign*, Nov. 1979, 102.

Every young woman is a child of destiny and every adult woman a powerful force for good.

JEFFREY R. HOLLAND, "TO YOUNG WOMEN," *ENSIGN,* NOV. 2005, 28.

A three-year-old had wandered off on an adventure, shedding his clothing as he went. When he realized he was lost as well as cold, he knocked at the home of this young woman. She saw a little boy standing on the step; he was wearing only soiled underwear and was crying his heart out. She took him in, and while they waited for the police to find his mother, she wrapped him in a blanket and held him on her lap and sang songs to him. She made him clown faces on home-dipped ice cream cones and drew pictures with him so he could surprise his mother. She made him feel marvelous.

When at last the boy's mother arrived, he started for the front door. Then suddenly he stopped, maybe remembering what a special time he had had with the young woman.

"Hey!" he asked. "Are you Heavenly Father's wife?"

The young woman was startled—and sobered. At last she replied, "No, but I am his daughter."

ELAINE A. CANNON, "VOICES," *NEW ERA,* JUL. 1980, 13.

*F*or the child there is magic in the midst of the mundane—watching Mother dance around the kitchen, taking a buggy ride wrapped up in her arms, trying to knead the bread dough just as she does, sharing a prayer, hearing her word of praise or encouragement. Such precious memories can be every mother's most enduring gift.

"Magical Moments," *Ensign*, Mar. 1985, 44.

*O*f all the creations of the Almighty there is none more beautiful, none more inspiring than a lovely daughter of God who walks in virtue with an understanding of why she should do so, who honors and respects her body as a thing sacred and divine, who cultivates her mind and constantly enlarges the horizon of her understanding, who nurtures her spirit with everlasting truth. God has given us a great and compelling trust.

GORDON B. HINCKLEY, "YOUTH IS THE SEASON," *NEW ERA*, SEP. 1988, 44.

The following incident occurred in a concentration camp during World War II

One afternoon we had to stand in line to receive our food and water rations. Our mother could barely stand, let alone walk, but she . . . stood in line with us, in obvious pain, leaning heavily on a stick. Seeing my mother like that fueled the hatred in my heart for those responsible . . . When I passed one of the officers . . . I threw my cup . . . in his face and spat at him.

Immediately a samurai sword was drawn toward me. Quickly my mother put her hands on the sword and pushed it away from me, cutting her hands . . .

"Please pick up your cup, Kitty, and apologize," she begged me softly. . . .

With great difficulty she bent and picked up the cup, then bowed deeply . . . She offered apologies in my name, telling him that I was only a child and had not acquired the discipline to master my emotions . . . "If there must be a punishment," she said, "I will take it for my child."

. . . The officer slowly put the sword back in its sheath, gently took the cup from my mother's hands, and filled it with water. "Woman, drink!" he said, and . . . my mother drank the water eagerly. He took the cup from her hands, filled it a second time, and offered it to my mother with both hands and a slight bow . . .

"It is I who must apologize to you for not recognizing the majesty of your womanhood," he said.

KITTY DE RUYTER, "A MOTHER'S LOVE," 1998, 19–20.

Countenance

Have ye received his image
in your countenances?

ALMA 5:14

Our outward appearance is a reflection of what we are on the inside. Our lives reflect that for which we seek. And if with all our hearts we truly seek to know the Savior and to be more like Him, we shall be, for He is our divine, eternal Brother. But He is more than that. He is our precious Savior, our dear Redeemer.

MARGARET D. NADAULD, "THE JOY OF WOMANHOOD," ENSIGN, NOV. 2000, 14.

repare yourselves to ennoble,
to enrich, and even to become the
heart and soul of the home. You may
bless others either as mothers or as legislators; as
leaders in the schoolroom or in the laboratory of
truth; at the hearth or at the crib side.

RUSSELL M. NELSON, "DAUGHTERS OF ZION," YOUNG WOMEN NEW ERA, NOV. 1985, 5.

The happiest women I know are those whose families would rather be home than any place else; whose children come bounding in after school to look for Mother to tell her about their activities of the day; who share the sorrows and joys and successes of those children and rejoice in their accomplishments; who glow with pride as their children take their places of leadership in political, business, and community life; and eventually share their love with grandchildren, whose response opens up a whole new world of rewarding satisfaction.

N. Eldon Tanner, "Happiness Is Home Centered," *Tambuli*, Feb. 1979, 1.

*M*otherhood is the one thing in all the world which most truly exemplifies the God-given virtues of creating and sacrificing. . . . The mother who, in compliance with eternal law, brings into the world an immortal spirit occupies first rank in the realm of creation.

DAVID O. MCKAY, *GOSPEL IDEALS*, 1953, 456.

Righteousness

Where spiritual things are concerned, as pertaining to all of the gifts of the Spirit, with reference to the receipt of revelation, the gaining of testimonies, and the seeing of visions, in all matters that pertain to godliness and holiness and which are brought to pass as a result of personal righteousness—in all these things men and women stand in a position of absolute equality before the Lord.

BRUCE R. McCONKIE, "OUR SISTERS FROM THE BEGINNING," ENSIGN, JAN. 1979, 61.

*S*he who can paint a masterpiece or write a book that will influence millions deserves the admiration and the plaudits of mankind; but she who rears successfully a family of healthy, beautiful sons and daughters, whose influence will be felt through generations to come, whose immortal souls will exert an influence throughout the ages long after paintings shall have faded, and books and statues shall have decayed or shall have been destroyed, deserves the highest honor that man can give, and the choicest blessings of God.

DAVID O. MCKAY, *GOSPEL IDEALS*, 1953, 453–54.

Greg K. Olsen

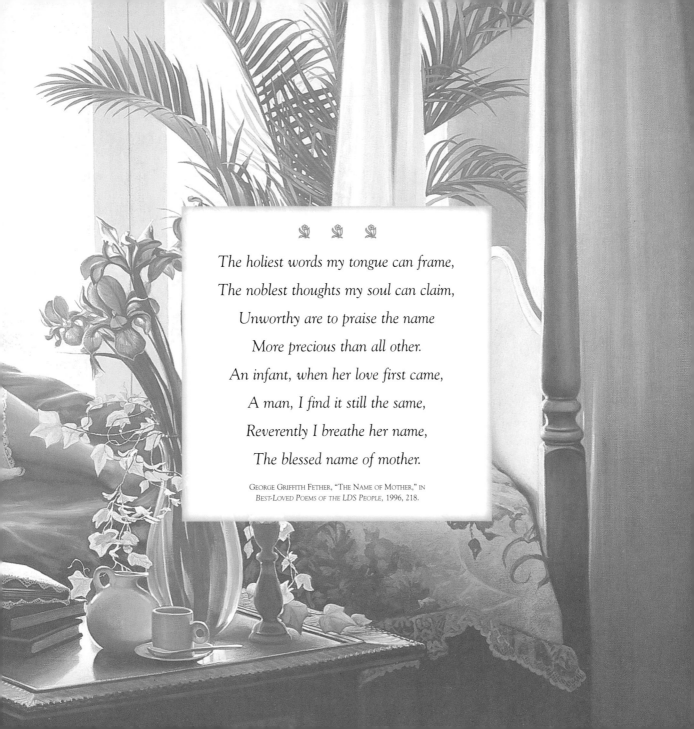

The holiest words my tongue can frame,

The noblest thoughts my soul can claim,

Unworthy are to praise the name

More precious than all other.

An infant, when her love first came,

A man, I find it still the same,

Reverently I breathe her name,

The blessed name of mother.

GEORGE GRIFFITH FETHER, "THE NAME OF MOTHER," IN
BEST-LOVED POEMS OF THE LDS PEOPLE, 1996, 218.

*G*od bless you my beloved sisters—you little girls whom we so much appreciate; you beautiful young women who dream wonderful dreams of the future; you who are not married and sometimes feel lonely, but who, I assure you, the Lord has not forgotten; those of you who carry the burdens of rearing families; those of you who are widowed or divorced; and you beautiful older women whom we so love and honor and respect. God

bless you with every righteous desire, with peace in your hearts and joy in your days, as daughters of God blessed with the light of his everlasting gospel.

GORDON B. HINCKLEY, "IF THOU ART FAITHFUL," *TAMBULI*, MAR. 1992, 3.

Many years ago when my oldest son was a very little boy, I found myself one warm summer night after supper frantically trying to finish bottling some fruit. . . . I began to peel and pit that fruit, when my two little boys appeared in the kitchen and announced that they were ready to say their prayers. [I answered,] "Now why don't you run in and say your prayers all alone and Mother will just keep on working at this fruit." David, the oldest planted his little feet firmly in front of me and asked, not unkindly, "But, Mommy, which is the most important, the prayers or fruit?"

HELEN LEE GOATES, CONFERENCE REPORT, MEXICO AND CENTRAL AMERICA AREA CONFERENCE 1972, 90–91.

From the beginning the women of the Christian church have shown their surpassing faith and devotion. Only one Apostle stood near the Cross while the Christ was crucified, but Mary, the mother, was there, and Mary Magdalene, and Mary, the mother of James and Joses, and the mother of Zebedee's children, and the women that followed Him from Galilee. It was Mary Magdalene who was first at the tomb when the Sabbath had ended, and to her Christ vouchsafed the first view to mortals of His resurrected body.

From that time until now woman has comforted and nursed the Church. She has borne more than half the burdens, she has made more than half the sacrifices, she has suffered the most of the heartaches and sorrows.

In the modern Church hers has been the abiding, unquestioning faith, the pure knowledge, that has enheartened the Priesthood and kept it going forward against all odds. Her loving trust, her loyal devotion were the faithful anchor that held when storms were fiercest.

J. REUBEN CLARK, JR., *CONFERENCE REPORT*, APR. 1940, 21.

often remember sitting in the sunlight as a child and my mother telling me how beautiful my hair looked in the sunshine. I remember her getting down on the carpet and rolling the ball to us. And I remember how we always loved to be in the kitchen with all the warm smells of cooking while she made chutneys and jams and told us about her grandparents.

MARGARET HAMSTEAD, "MAGICAL MOMENTS," *ENSIGN*, MAR. 1985, 44.

Each of us has a vital role, even a sacred mission to perform as a daughter of Zion. . . . It is our destiny to rejoice as we fill the earth with greater kindness and gentleness, greater love and compassion, greater sympathy and empathy than have ever been known before. It is time to give ourselves to the Master and allow Him to lead us into fruitful fields where we can enrich a world filled with darkness and misery.

Mary Ellen W. Smoot, "Rejoice, Daughters of Zion," *Ensign*, Nov. 1999, 94.

Y ou can recognize . . . women who are grateful to be daughters of God by their attitudes. They know the errand of angels is given to women, and they desire to be on God's errand, to love His children and minister to them; to teach them the doctrines of salvation; . . . to deliver His messages. They understand they can bless their Father's children in their homes and neighborhoods and beyond. . . . Women who are grateful to be daughters of God bring glory to His name.

Margaret D. Nadauld, "What You Are Meant to Be,"
New Era, Oct. 2002, 42.

Attitude

he most perfect ideal in
the art of healing is the
mother whose tender and gracious love asserts
itself in taking away the sting of a deserved or an
undeserved punishment. How her love heals
every wound! How quick her caresses bind up
and soothe! The example of her life is the
wisdom which love teaches.

JOSEPH F. SMITH, GOSPEL DOCTRINE, 1939, 264.

O Jerusalem . . . how often would I have gathered
thy children together, even as a hen gathereth
her chickens under her wings, and ye would not!

MATT. 23:37

❋   ❋   ❋

I believe that every mother has the right to . . . know what to do in her family and in her sphere and that mother and every mother possessing that spirit has the gift of revelation, the gift of inspiration . . . a gift of God to them, to govern their households and lead their children in the path of righteousness and truth.

JOSEPH F. SMITH, ADDRESS AT THE HOME OF A. W. McCUNE, 14 NOV. 1913.

When the real history of mankind is fully disclosed, will it feature the echoes of gunfire or the shaping sound of lullabies? The great armistices made by military men or the peacemaking of women in homes and in neighborhoods? Will what happened in cradles and kitchens prove to be more controlling than what happened in congresses?

NEAL A. MAXWELL, "THE WOMEN OF GOD," *ENSIGN*, MAY 1978, 10–11.

At is natural for females to have feelings of charity and benevolence. . . . If you live up to these principles, how great and glorious will be your reward in the celestial kingdom! If you live up to your privileges, the angels cannot be restrained from being your associates.

JOSEPH SMITH, *HISTORY OF THE CHURCH*, 4:605.

Intelligence

"Whatever principle of intelligence we attain unto in this life, it will rise with us in the resurrection." I should like to say to every one of you sisters here that as a member of The Church of Jesus Christ of Latter-day Saints, you have an obligation to refine and improve your minds and your skills, for each of you is a daughter of God with a divine birthright and with an obligation to grow toward his stature.

GORDON B. HINCKLEY, "FOR GIRLS ONLY," *NEW ERA*, NOV. 1971, 35.

2–3
Mother and daughter at piano engraving from *Music: A Pictorial Archive of Woodcuts & Engravings* © 1980 Dover Publications, Inc.

I Feel My Savior's Love © Greg Olsen by arrangement with Mill Pond Press.

4–5
Prelude © Greg Olsen by arrangement with Mill Pond Press.

6–7
Children of the World © Greg Olsen by arrangement with Mill Pond Press.

8–9
Floral engraving from *Old-Fashioned Floral Bouquets* © 1997 Dover Publications, Inc.

One Man's Trash Is Another Man's Treasure © Greg Olsen by arrangement with Mill Pond Press.

10–11
He Is Risen © Greg Olsen by arrangement with Mill Pond Press.

Young woman engraving from *Women: A Pictorial Archive from Nineteenth-Century Sources* © 1982 Dover Publications, Inc.

12–13
Dress Rehearsal © Greg Olsen by arrangement with Mill Pond Press.

Floral engraving from *Old-Fashioned Floral Bouquets* © 1997 Dover Publications, Inc.

14–15
Lost and Found © Greg Olsen by arrangement with Mill Pond Press.

16–17
Scales engraving from *2001 Decorative Cuts and Ornaments* © 1988 Dover Publications, Inc.

The Sower © Greg Olsen by arrangement with Mill Pond Press.

The Harvester © Greg Olsen by arrangement with Mill Pond Press.

18–19
Detail from *Timothy Reading Sacred Writings with His Mother and Grandmother* Fig 303 from *The New Testament: A Pictorial Archive from Nineteenth-Century Sources* © 1986 Dover Publications, Inc.

Teach the Children of Men by the Power of My Spirit by Greg Olsen © Intellectual Reserve, Inc.

20–21
Abide with Me © Greg Olsen by arrangement with Mill Pond Press.

22–23
After the Masquerade © Greg Olsen by arrangement with Mill Pond Press.

24–25
Floral engraving from *Old-Fashioned Floral Bouquets* © 1997 Dover Publications, Inc.

Lost No More © Greg Olsen by arrangement with Mill Pond Press.

26–27
Melodies Remembered © Greg Olsen by arrangement with Mill Pond Press.

Woman playing violin engraving from *Music: A Pictorial Archive of Woodcuts & Engravings* © 1980 Dover Publications, Inc.

28–29
King of Kings © Greg Olsen by arrangement with Mill Pond Press.

Floral engraving from *Old-Fashioned Floral Bouquets* © 1997 Dover Publications, Inc.

30–31
Winter Quarters © Greg Olsen by arrangement with Mill Pond Press.

32–33
Floral engraving from *Old-Fashioned Floral Bouquets* © 1997 Dover Publications, Inc.

I Love New Yorkies © Greg Olsen by arrangement with Mill Pond Press.

34–35
Forever and Ever © Greg Olsen by arrangement with Mill Pond Press.

Woman with arms around son and infant on floor engraving from *Music: A Pictorial Archive of Woodcuts & Engravings* © 1980 Dover Publications, Inc.

36–37
Song of Praise © Greg Olsen by arrangement with Mill Pond Press.

38–39
Side by Side © Greg Olsen by arrangement with Mill Pond Press.

40–41
Heavenly Hands © Greg Olsen by arrangement with Mill Pond Press.

Floral engraving from *Old-Fashioned Floral Bouquets* © 1997 Dover Publications, Inc.

42–43
Christ Raising the Daughter of Jairus by Greg Olsen © Intellectual Reserve, Inc.

Hannah's Prayer by Julius Schnorr von Carolsfeld from *Treasury of Bible Illustrations: Old and New Testaments* © 1999 Dover Publications, Inc.

44–45
Heaven Sent © Greg Olsen by arrangement with Mill Pond Press.

46–47
Formal Luncheon © Greg Olsen by arrangement with Mill Pond Press.

48–49
Floral engraving from *Old-Fashioned Floral Bouquets* © 1997 Dover Publications, Inc.

Front Porch Tea Party © Greg Olsen by arrangement with Mill Pond Press.

50–51
Young woman and child engraving from *Women: A Pictorial Archive from Nineteenth-Century Sources* © 1982 Dover Publications, Inc.

In His Light © Greg Olsen by arrangement with Mill Pond Press.

52–53
Floral engraving from *Old-Fashioned Floral Bouquets* © 1997 Dover Publications, Inc.

Pots and Pans Band © Greg Olsen by arrangement with Mill Pond Press.

54–55
Denim to Lace © Greg Olsen by arrangement with Mill Pond Press.

56–57
Floral engraving from *Old-Fashioned Floral Bouquets* © 1997 Dover Publications, Inc.

In His Constant Care © Greg Olsen by arrangement with Mill Pond Press.

58–59
Portrait of a young woman engraving from *Women: A Pictorial Archive from Nineteenth-Century Sources* © 1982 Dover Publications, Inc.

Daddy's Little Girl © Greg Olsen by arrangement with Mill Pond Press.

60–61
Precious in His Sight © Greg Olsen by arrangement with Mill Pond Press.

Floral engraving from *Old-Fashioned Floral Bouquets* © 1997 Dover Publications, Inc.

62–63
Fairy Tales © Greg Olsen by arrangement with Mill Pond Press.

64–65
Angels of Christmas © Greg Olsen by arrangement with Mill Pond Press.

Floral engraving from *Old-Fashioned Floral Bouquets* © 1997 Dover Publications, Inc.

66–67
Contemplative young woman engraving from *Women: A Pictorial Archive from Nineteenth-Century Sources* © 1982 Dover Publications, Inc.

Fountains of My Youth © Greg Olsen by arrangement with Mill Pond Press.

68–69
Floral engraving from *Old-Fashioned Floral Bouquets* © 1997 Dover Publications, Inc.

Cream and Sugar © Greg Olsen by arrangement with Mill Pond Press.

70–71
Mother's Love © Greg Olsen by arrangement with Mill Pond Press.

72–73
Delicate Balance © Greg Olsen by arrangement with Mill Pond Press.

Floral engraving from *Old-Fashioned Floral Bouquets* © 1997 Dover Publications, Inc.

The Russian Flower Vendor © Greg Olsen by arrangement with Mill Pond Press.

74–75
Don't Forget to Pray © Greg Olsen by arrangement with Mill Pond Press.

Woman Taken in Adultery before Jesus from *The New Testament: A Pictorial Archive from Nineteenth-Century Sources* © 1986 Dover Publications, Inc.

76–77
Be Not Afraid © Greg Olsen by arrangement with Mill Pond Press.

Floral engraving from *Old-Fashioned Floral Bouquets* © 1997 Dover Publications, Inc.

78–79
Summerhouse © Greg Olsen by arrangement with Mill Pond Press.

80–81
Light of the World © Greg Olsen by arrangement with Mill Pond Press.

Woman carrying wheat engraving from *Women: A Pictorial Archive from Nineteenth-Century Sources* © 1982 Dover Publications, Inc.

82–83
Women engaged in rural activity engraving from *Women: A Pictorial Archive from Nineteenth-Century Sources* © 1982 Dover Publications, Inc.

Confidant © Greg Olsen by arrangement with Mill Pond Press.

84–85
Forgiven © Greg Olsen by arrangement with Mill Pond Press.

86–87
O Jerusalem © Greg Olsen by arrangement with Mill Pond Press.

88–89
Little Girls Will Mothers Be © Greg Olsen by arrangement with Mill Pond Press.

Floral engraving from *Old-Fashioned Floral Bouquets* © 1997 Dover Publications, Inc.

90–91
The Messenger © Greg Olsen by arrangement with Mill Pond Press.

92–93
Portrait of an elderly woman engraving from *Women: A Pictorial Archive from Nineteenth-Century Sources* © 1982 Dover Publications, Inc.

Once Upon a Time © Greg Olsen by arrangement with Mill Pond Press.